W9-AFS-722

American Community

Early American Villages

Raymond Bial

Children's Press®
A Division of Scholastic Inc.
New York   Toronto   London   Auckland   Sydney
Mexico City   New Delhi   Hong Kong
Danbury, Connecticut

Library of Congress Cataloging-in-Publication Data

Bial, Raymond.
  Early American villages / by Raymond Bial.
       p. cm. — (American community)
  Includes bibliographical references and index.
  ISBN 0–516–23704–7 (lib. bdg.) 0–516–25076–0 (pbk.)
  1. United States—Social life and customs—To 1775—Juvenile
literature. 2. Villages—United States—History—Juvenile literature.
3. Community life—United States—History—Juvenile literature. 4.
City and town life—United States—History—Juvenile literature. 5.
United States—History—Colonial period, ca. 1600–1775—Juvenile
literature. I. Title.
  E162.B53 2004
  973.2—dc22

                                                    2004005088

Cover design by Doug Andersen
Map by Robert Cronan

Photographs © 2004 : Colonial Williamsburg Foundation, Williamsburg, Virginia: front
cover, 20, 21; Corbis Images/Kelly-Mooney Photography: 41; Hulton|Archive/Getty
Images: 27 right, 43; Library of Congress: 25; North Wind Picture Archives: 13 right; Old
Sturbridge Village: 17 left (Chuck Kidd/50.C78.36.1), 19 (Thomas Neill/80.L56.1995.9.1);
Photri Inc./Lani Howe: 29; Raymond Bial: back cover, 1, 5, 9 left, 9 right, 11, 13 left, 14,
15 bottom, 15 top, 16, 17 bottom right, 17 top right, 22 bottom, 22 top, 23, 24, 26, 27 left,
28, 30, 31, 32, 33, 35, 36, 37, 38, 39, 40; Stock Boston/Cary Wolinsky: 6.

Contents

The Colonies 4

Villages 7

Craftsmen 14

One-Room Schools 18

Chores and Community Gatherings 21

Houses 26

Gardens and Orchards 34

Outbuildings 36

From Colonies to Young Nation 40

Glossary *42*

Time Line *43*

Find Out More *44*

Index *46*

About the Author *48*

The Colonies

In 1607, a ship landed on the coast of what is now Virginia. With the consent of King James I of England, the people aboard had ventured across the Atlantic Ocean to start a new life in a new land. Swinging axes, these colonists, as they were known, cleared a patch of forest near the shore and built a small village. Here in Virginia, they hoped to establish a colony, or territory ruled by another country. Named for the English king, Jamestown became the first permanent English settlement in North America.

The colonists at Jamestown built one-room, timber-frame cottages. To make the walls, they plastered woven branches with mud in a style called wattle-and-daub. They laid reeds to make a thatched roof that readily shed the rain. They built stone or brick chimneys for cooking and heat in the winter. The cluster of mud huts was situated within a fort with high, thick walls. The fort was needed for protection against attacks from the Native American tribes on whose lands the English colonists had settled.

The first Jamestown colonists searched for gold in the forests. However, they never found any gold and nearly starved in their early years—until the Powhatan Indians traded food

In 1607, English colonists of the London Company founded Jamestown, Virginia, where they built sturdy homes.

Settling at Plymouth, Massachusetts, the Pilgrims made peace with the Wampanoag Indians and celebrated the first Thanksgiving in 1621.

and taught them to plant corn. As more people arrived in Virginia, the English established other communities in this southern colony. The colonists began to grow tobacco, which over time brought great prosperity to the region.

Not all colonists wanted to become wealthy. In 1620, the Pilgrims landed at Plymouth Rock in what became the colony of Massachusetts. Some Pilgrims belonged to a strict religious group called the Puritans who were persecuted in England. Working together, they established the small village of Plymouth. As this village prospered, other Puritans immigrated to Massachusetts. Over time, some people broke away from the Puritans and established communities in Rhode Island and other parts of New England. All of these groups sought a place where they could freely practice their religion.

Along the Hudson River, the Dutch established New Netherland in what later became New York. In 1682, another religious group settled in a colony that was named Pennsylvania after their leader William Penn. These people were called the Quakers, because they often shook, or quaked, during their meetings. Persecuted in England, these peaceful people established the town of Philadelphia and then other villages on the frontier in the middle part of the Atlantic coast.

English colonies were also established in Maryland, Delaware, and farther south in the Carolinas and Georgia. For two hundred years, thousands of people from other countries also left their homes and sailed across the Atlantic Ocean. Germans, Scandinavians, Irish, Scotch-Irish, and many other immigrants settled among the Quakers and Dutch in the Middle Colonies. Others sought freedom or fortunes in New England or one of the southern colonies.

Even if they came as servants, colonists could at least hope to earn a living and someday own a house and a little land. They longed for a new life in the colonies along the eastern seaboard, which would in time become the United States of America.

Villages

Early Americans had three resources not available in Europe. They had abundant wood, plenty of land, and many swift streams to furnish power for mills. One man said, there was "good living for those that love good fires." Yet the forest supplied more than firewood for warmth and cooking. Trees could be harvested for logs and lumber to build homes, shops, and fences for homesteads and villages.

To establish a village, people first cleared the thick forest and built a sawmill along the river. The flowing water powered the gears and large saws, which turned logs into piles of flat boards. Carpenters used these boards to build houses and shops. An enterprising man might also start a brickworks in the settlement. The brickmaker dug clay from a nearby river-bank or hillside. He shaped the clay into bricks, which were hardened by firing in an oven called a kiln. The bricks were used to build fireplaces and chimneys, and sometimes houses.

People also built a gristmill along a stream to grind corn, wheat, barley, and oats into flour. The gristmill had machinery —wooden gears, rods, and a grindstone—that easily ground large amounts of grain. Water flowed over the paddles of a wooden wheel, making it turn. The gears and rods connected to the waterwheel rotated and turned a heavy grindstone, which ground the grain into flour. An experienced miller was

In New England villages, the gristmill was one of the first and most important businesses established by the Pilgrims and other colonists.

Operated by gears, sawmills produced lumber, which colonists used to build houses, shops, and other buildings.

needed to run this kind of mill. He had to know how to grind the grain properly and repair all the machinery. Until they had a gristmill, people had to pound their grain by hand with a mortar and pestle. However, once the gristmill was established, people took their grain there to be ground into flour or sold.

In New England, **surveyors** often laid out the village with a common, or green, in the middle of the community. They built a **meetinghouse** on the common, where people discussed local matters and voted. Meetings were not fully democratic, since women couldn't vote, or even voice an opinion. Servants and working men who owned no property also could not take part in these meetings. Yet the meetinghouse was the center of the community. Everyone met there regularly for church—even though the services were long and the benches were uncomfortable.

Notices were nailed to the meetinghouse door, where people would be sure to see them. These included notices of town meetings, cattle sales, lists of village officers, wedding announcements, and other local news. Outside there were stepping stones or horse-blocks to make it easier to dismount, since many people rode horses to the meetinghouse. Often, a whipping post and stocks where people were punished for crimes were placed by the meetinghouse.

Villagers might also share grazing lands just outside the village. A cow herder, or "cow-keep," was hired by the village to watch over all the cows. The cow-keep was often paid in butter or cheese. This cooperative task allowed the busy farmers, craftsmen, and shop owners of the village to go about other work. Typically, "a chosen proper youngster" walked through the village at dawn blowing a horn to call the cattle. The cattle followed the boy to the pastures where they grazed until sunset. The boy then returned the cattle safely to the village, often sounding his horn to let their owners know that it was now milking time.

Occasionally, shepherds were also hired to watch over flocks of sheep on common lands. Whether for cattle or sheep, these plots of land needed good fences and villages often hired fence-viewers to make sure that the fences on the "great lotts" were in good repair. Each person had to help maintain the fence—either through his own work or by payment to another person. Usually, a person was responsible for a twenty-foot

Just as colonists cooperated on many large tasks, such as corn huskings, they also shared grazing lands for their cattle and sheep.

section of fence for each animal that he owned. If the fence was in poor repair and cattle got out, the owner of that section was responsible for the damage. However, if it was determined that the fence was in good repair and the cattle unruly, the owner of the cattle had to pay for any damage to gardens and crops.

Merchants, including storekeepers, bankers, and tavern keepers, opened businesses around the common or along a main street. The tavern keeper (or the blacksmith) often operated a shelter for horses called a **livery stable**. Located in the center of the village, the general store was a favorite gathering place for people. Amid the smell of spices, people shared news. They discussed politics and the weather, along with gardening and crops. Children liked to visit the general store to buy rock candy and other sweets. Storekeepers stocked items made by local craftsmen and they imported pots and pans, guns, cloth, and spices from England. The shelves of this store were also crammed with groceries. People traded items from their own homestead, such as eggs and butter, for cloth, sugar, molasses, spices, and coffee. They also bartered for glassware, gunpowder, and many other goods.

The shelves of the general store were lined with useful goods, either made by local craftsmen or shipped in from Europe.

The local newspaper was very important to the village. Just four pages long, the newspaper still took a long time to print because all the type had to be set by hand. The newspaper editor tried to know everything about everyone in the village. He published news and covered social events in the village. The newspaper included notices about deaths, births, and weddings. It also published advertisements for goods, services, and property. The editor sometimes printed **broadsides**, which were advertising posters, or signs, for businesses. He might also publish books, including **almanacs**. These yearly publications featured information and advice about the

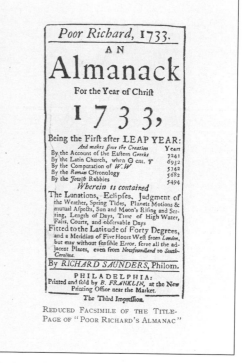

Colonial villages had newspapers or printing shops that published advertising posters called broadsides and books called almanacs.

weather, planting times for crops, and practical advice about life. Benjamin Franklin—who was a newspaperman as well as inventor, philosopher, and political leader—published a popular almanac.

Some communities also relied on a town crier for the latest news. As he walked around the village, he called out recent events to anyone within earshot. The town crier also announced meetings and other public events. He had the most current and interesting news, and he was especially important if the village had no newspaper.

Craftsmen

The village was a center for skilled craftsmen, or artisans, as well as shopkeepers. These people included carpenters, who built houses for people, and cabinetmakers who made furniture for the homes. Cabinetmakers used many kinds of hand tools. Some had specialized tasks, such as the **joiner**, a woodworker who fitted pieces of wood together to make furniture. A turner specialized in using a **lathe**, which was a machine that turned

The blacksmith crafted many useful iron tools and other objects that early Americans could not make for themselves.

wood. With sharp chisels, the turner then shaped the wood into legs for chairs and tables.

The blacksmith had one of the most important jobs in the village. He made essential items, such as horseshoes, nails, hinges, latches, and tools for family households and farms. He heated iron until it was red hot and soft. Gripping the iron with tongs, he hammered it into shape on an anvil. He might have to heat and hammer the horseshoe or other object several times before he got it into the right shape. He then dipped the object into cold water. It sizzled as it cooled and hardened again. Sometimes blacksmiths made objects of **cast-iron** in which melted metal was poured into molds. Other artisans shaped metal by hand to make **wrought iron** gates and fences with fancy designs.

Many other craftsmen worked with metal. The tinsmith made everyday objects, such as pitchers, mugs, and candleholders. Other workers were skilled in pewter, which they crafted into dishes for tableware, or silver for jewelry. Coopers made buckets and barrels from slats of wood. Wheelwrights made wheels for buggies and wagons.

Tinsmiths cut and shaped sheets of thin metal into many useful household goods, such as drinking cups, pitchers, and storage boxes.

A cooper specialized in making sturdy, watertight buckets and barrels from wooden slats.

A craftsman, known as a potter, dug clay from a nearby riverbank. He turned the clay on a wheel, shaping it into cups, bowls, pitchers, and other dishes.

Potters dug clay from riverbanks and shaped useful pots and cups on a round wheel in village shops. Most pottery, or earthenware, was simple and useful, although a few artisans crafted porcelain dishes from a fine white clay. The tanner bought animal hides from the butcher and local farmers, and turned them into soft leather through a process called tanning. The shoemaker then purchased cowhides from the tanner. He cut the cowhide into pieces, which he shaped and sewed into shoes and boots. Working at large looms, weavers made textiles, such as rugs for floors and tapestries for wall decorations, in family homes. In some communities, there were also broom makers and other craftsmen who supplied the community with everyday objects.

Many shops had an **apprentice**, who was learning the skills of the craftsman, or artisan. The apprentice was often indentured. Many people longed to come to America, but could not afford the cost of the sea voyage. So they made indentures, or contracts, with employers in the colonies. The employers paid for their trip, and the indentured worked as apprentices, farm hands, or house servants until their debt

The shoemaker cut pieces of leather from thick cowhides, which he shaped and sewed into shoes for everyone in the village.

Weavers made different kinds of fabrics, or textiles, including rugs, tapestries, and bed coverings.

Under the instruction of a skilled cooper, this young apprentice is learning how to shave wooden slats for buckets and barrels.

was repaid—often as long as seven years. About a third of all immigrants came as indentured servants, and in the Chesapeake Bay region as many as 40 percent.

Usually a young boy, the apprentice received room and board, but no pay. Living in the master's house, the apprentice often came to be treated like an adopted son in the family. However, some masters could be very cruel. They beat their apprentices, gave them little food, and worked them for long hours, trying to get as much work out of them as possible. An apprentice worked for several years and left after he had completed his training and indenture. He could then take over his master's business or open his own shop in a nearby village.

One-Room Schools

Schools were established in many early American villages. School was held in the late autumn to spring, since many students had to work on their family's farm from spring planting through fall harvesting. Girls usually attended through sixth grade, while boys continued until eighth grade. Only a few students went on to college.

Often located at the edge of town, the school building had just one room. The children all attended class in this one room and the teacher—schoolmaster or schoolmistress—simply assigned work by grade. Students learned reading, writing, and arithmetic, which is now called math. The children also helped take care of the school. They carried in firewood, swept the floor, and wiped down the blackboard. They filled buckets with water for drinking and for washing their hands and faces.

Since paper was expensive, children usually wrote their spelling, reading, and arithmetic lessons with chalk on slate boards.

During recess, children enjoyed playing games, such as rolling a hoop over the ground with a stick.

Students often wrote on slate boards with chalk, since paper was scarce and expensive. Teachers gave them an arithmetic problem, which they worked out on the slate. Or they said the words out loud, which the students had to spell correctly on the slate. After the teacher reviewed the answer on the slate, the student wiped the slate clean.

The teacher sometimes lived in a back room of the school building or in a small house next door. However, the teacher usually boarded with the family of one of the students. Teachers were very strict. They made students stand in the corner with a dunce cap on their head if they didn't do their schoolwork. If students misbehaved they might have their fingers whacked, or even their behinds whipped with a hickory stick.

Children worked hard in class, but they especially loved recess. They ate lunches brought from home and then enjoyed freetime to play. They took turns on a swing hanging from the branch of a large tree in the schoolyard. Or they played hide and seek, tag, and ball games. When the teacher rang a hand bell, they went back into the building and worked hard at their lessons.

Children didn't have homework, because they had chores at home at the end of the day.

Chores and Community Gatherings

Everyone in the family helped around the household. Girls fed the chickens, gathered eggs, and drew water from the well or spring in the yard. They learned to mend clothing, make candles, and look after the other children. From an early age, they helped their mothers harvesting in the garden and preparing meals at the fireplace.

Boys milked the family cow and fed the pigs. They chopped and carried firewood into the house—which was no small task. A house with just one fireplace burned about fifteen to twenty cords of wood a year. A cord was a stack of firewood four feet wide, four feet high, and eight feet long. From a young age, boys learned how to yoke and harness a team of oxen. They helped with planting, cultivation, and harvesting

Among their many chores, children pulled weeds in the garden, harvested vegetables, and shucked fresh sweet corn.

Families raised sheep for wool, which was made into warm clothing, and grew flax, which was woven into a fine cloth called linen.

Early Americans made candles to light their homes by methodically dipping wicks into melted tallow or beeswax.

corn, wheat, flax, and other crops. Flax was important not as food, but in making a cloth called linen, which women sewed into clothing. Boys also helped to build and repair fences.

Mothers, fathers, and children worked long hours everyday. However, families still needed the help of friends and neighbors for many work activities that were difficult or impossible for them to do on their own. So, people often came together for major tasks, such as house raisings and stone haulings. People worked hard, but there was also plenty of laughter and gossip, along with an abundance of food—not only hearty meat dishes, but also sweet cakes and pies.

Small groups of women frequently gathered and helped each other with backbreaking tasks. Together, they dipped candles, made soap, wove rag carpets, made apple butter, and undertook other burdensome chores. Women dreaded their yearly house cleaning. So, they got together for "spring cleaning." They would thoroughly clean one woman's house and then move on to another's house the next week until everyone's home was neat and tidy.

Girls and women got together to make candles from beeswax or they melted animal fat into tallow. They often added ginger, honey, bayberries, or other ingredients so that the burning candle had a pleasant fragrance. To make candles, they re-peatedly dipped each end of a string called a wick into the hot tallow or beeswax until they were coated. The pairs of tapered candles were then hung on pegs to dry. Girls and women also formed candles by pouring tallow or beeswax into metal molds.

Women also made their own soap, usually in the autumn when there was plenty of animal fat. Throughout the year they collected rainwater, which was allowed to seep through fire-place ashes to make a harsh liquid called lye. They had to be

Girls and women made their own soap, which was cut into thick bars used to wash clothes and dishes, as well as hands and faces.

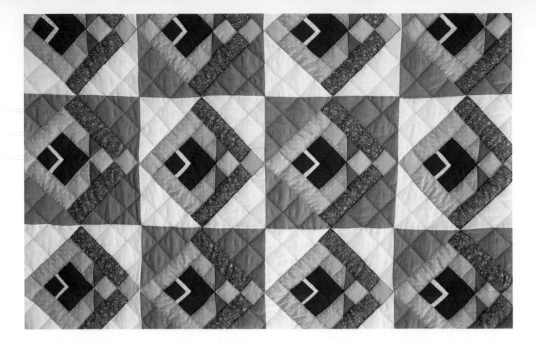

Early American women often gathered to undertake many large, difficult tasks, such as making quilts for families.

very careful with lye, which would burn if just a few drops were splashed on their skin. They mixed the lye with tallow and often added spices for fragrance. The mixture was poured into shallow wooden boxes and allowed to cool and harden overnight. The slabs of soap were then cut into bars.

Many women enjoyed quilting bees in which they met in each other's homes and sewed bed coverings called quilts. They patched together two layers of cloth, which they then sewed together with a soft, warm material called batting in between. Quilts usually had striking colors and designs. In every home, people slept under several quilts because the unheated bedrooms became very chilly in the winter. Women often got together to make a quilt for special occasions—when a baby was born or a couple was about to be married. This quilt became a cherished gift, which was often handed down from one generation to another in the family.

Men, women, and children also helped each other during seasonal tasks, such as corn shucking and apple paring in the autumn. When the weather got cold, they gathered to butcher hogs. They hung hams, sausage, and bacon in a smokehouse. Women pickled and canned some of the meat. They butchered chickens whenever needed for Sunday dinner or a family visit. In the spring, people often tapped maple trees for their sap, which was collected in a metal can. They boiled down the sap to make thick, sweet maple syrup.

The Puritans tended to be very strict and devoted their free time to worship. However, throughout the year, many early Americans enjoyed social occasions, such as weekly dances in the meetinghouse or a local barn. Women and men put on their finest clothes and looked forward to a night of music, food, and fun.

This young woman is gathering holly to decorate the house for the holidays.

Houses

The first colonists lived in rough-hewn cabins and mud-walled cottages. Scandinavian and German settlers in Pennsylvania built log cabins like those in their native European countries. As early Americans prospered, however, carpenters built larger homes with several rooms and often two stories. Most were made of timber-frames covered with narrow boards called clapboards. In the early years, these houses were left unpainted. Other houses were built of sturdy bricks or stones.

Split wooden boards were used to make shingled roofs to shed the rain and snow. Many early American homes had a simple pitched roof like an upside down V. Others, which came to be known as colonial homes, had a gambrel, or double-pitched roof. The roofs of a popular New England style that sloped over back rooms came to be called a saltbox, which it resembled. Roofs on New England homes tended to be steep so the snow would slide off.

In the South, roofs extended farther over the walls. This overhang provided more shade to keep the house cooler in the

Left unpainted, the clapboards of early American homes weathered to a gray color in the sun and rain.

With its roof sloping over the back rooms, the saltbox became a popular house style in New England.

summer. Southern houses also had high ceilings and porches where people could sit out in the hot evenings. In Virginia and Maryland, people lived farther apart and did not build many towns. Life came to center on large farms called plantations. Plantations became the communities in the south that were more important than villages and towns. On these plantations, people built large, expensive homes called mansions. In later colonial years, slaves, who were brought from Africa against their will, worked on the plantations—in fields, workshops and homes. They lived in cabins or shacks behind the big house and near the fields, where they formed their own

On southern plantations, slaves not only did most of the daily work, but they also formed their own communities.

Silhouettes of family members were framed and hung on the walls. This was a simple and inexpensive way of decorating early American homes.

communities. The first African-American slaves were brought to Virginia in 1619. Their numbers grew steadily until they undertook most of the work in the fields and homes.

Whatever their style, the first American homes had small windows, because glass was expensive. People used paper soaked in linseed oil from the flax plant as windowpanes. These oiled paper windows let only a little yellowish light into the rooms. Later, as people prospered, they had windows made with glass imported from England or Holland and doors with iron hinges and latches. Only wealthy colonists brought furniture with them—shipping costs were too high. Early homes had little more than chairs or benches, usually grouped around the fire where people gathered. However, over time, American cabinetmakers made comfortable and stylish furniture for these homes.

There were few decorations in homes. Photography had not yet been invented, and only wealthy people could afford paintings of the family. So people often made **silhouettes** of family members, which they put in picture frames and hung on the wall. Silhouettes were profiles, or side views of people, cut out of dark material and mounted against a light background. Women also enjoyed fancy sewing called **embroidery** and needlepoint, in which they stitched designs on cloth, leather, or paper. They sometimes hung their framed needlework on the walls of their homes.

In early America, the mother was in charge of the household. She was responsible for caring for the children, growing and gathering, preserving, and cooking foods. Daughters helped with many chores—gathering eggs, churning butter, peeling potatoes, and baking bread. In rich families, the mother only planned meals, which were then prepared by slaves or **indentured** servants.

The Kitchen. The kitchen was the most important room in early American homes. It was usually located at the back of the home, although in the South, people usually had two kitchens —one for winter and another for summer. The summer kitchen was often a separate building because the cooking fire made the house too hot. Sometimes, it was connected to the house by a covered walkway called a breezeway. Homes also had a small storeroom called a pantry next to the kitchen. Here,

At a young age, girls became very skilled with the arts of embroidery and other fine needlework.

Girls and women had to be very careful of their long dresses as they tended the fire and cooked meals for their families.

German colonists kept sauerkraut, meaning "sour cabbage," pickles in large jars, and coleslaw or koolslaa. They might also keep a few cookies, from the Dutch word koekje, in the pantry, along with vegetables, dried herbs, and household dishes.

The fireplace was the heart of the kitchen. Women needed tools for handling the fire—a shovel to remove ashes, tongs to shift logs, and bellows to fan the embers and flames—along with cooking utensils. They cooked with a pan called a spider, which had legs that raised it over the hot coals. The spider had a long handle so that women in ankle-length dresses didn't have to get too close to the fire. Women used a metal rod called a **lug pole** for hanging pots over the fire. Pots for stews and soups were hung from metal hooks called trammels on an iron crane that could be swung over the fire. Women used trammels of different lengths to move the pot closer to or farther away from the fire. Women roasted meat over the fire on a long iron rod called a spit. They turned the meat on a dog wheel or jack. They boiled water in heavy kettles.

Sometimes an oven was built into the side of the chimney to bake bread. The oven had an iron door to keep it hot inside. Other times cooks used a Dutch oven instead. These were large, heavy cast iron pots that were made with lids so hot coals could be scooped over the kettle so the cornbread, called Johnnycakes, or other breads baked evenly.

Foods. Early colonists usually ate a thick corn mush or oatmeal porridge for breakfast. Served between noon and three o'clock in the afternoon, dinner was their main meal. People generally ate a meat and vegetable stew or fried pork and bacon. They ate with a knife and fork, called cutlery, scooping food with a knife instead of a spoon. Food was often served onto pewter plates from wooden trays called **trenchers**, and people drank from tall mugs called **tankards**.

With a knife and fork, people ate food from metal plates and drank milk and other drinks from tin cups (above), or from large mugs called tankards.

Beds often had tall posts with a canopy overhead. They were often heated with warming pans during the cold winter months.

Native Americans introduced tasty new foods to the colonists, especially corn, beans, squash, and pumpkins. In New England, colonists cooked beans in soups and stews. In Boston, they made baked beans that are still popular today. People cooked and mashed pumpkin to bake delicious pies. They also dried pumpkin slices, which kept well. However, corn became the most vital new food. It could be easily grown and used in many dishes. People ate fresh corn on the cob and pounded corn into a meal that was used in breads and porridge. In the South, people boiled corn into a soft, white porridge called *grits*.

In the Carolinas, people came to love sweet potatoes, which could be prepared in many different ways. The whole root was sometimes roasted in hot ashes and eaten while hot. It could also be boiled and mashed into puddings, pies, and pancakes—or even baked into breads.

Early Americans loved sweets. They bought sugar in large white cones called loaves, which weighed eight to ten pounds. But sugar was expensive. The loaf was locked up and taken out only when needed. Pieces were carefully cut off with special sugar shears. The loaf might last a year. Because people couldn't always afford to buy sugar, they also used molasses, honey, and maple sugar as sweeteners.

Bedchambers. Early American homes had sleeping rooms called bedchambers. The parents slept in the largest room, and children slept in smaller rooms, where they kept dolls, rocking horses, and other toys. Cabinetmakers crafted many kinds of beds, including a four-poster that had tall posts at each corner. A rope key, or bed wrench, was used to tighten the rows of crisscrossed ropes that served as bedsprings. They also had trundle beds that could be pushed under a larger bed to save space. Bedchambers were often cold, even if the room had a fireplace. So, people used a **warming pan** to heat their beds before they retired for the night. This flat, closed metal pan had a long handle. The pan was filled with hot coals and closed with a lid that allowed heat to escape. People swept the warming pan between the sheets to make the bed warm and snug.

Bedchambers did not have closets. People kept their clothes in chests of drawers. Cabinetmakers sometimes built these chests with secret compartments for hiding money and jewelry. People also had a washstand to wash their faces and

Bedrooms had a water bowl, jug, and soap, where people could wash their hands and faces before going to sleep at night.

hands before they went to bed. This wooden stand held a bowl, water jug, and soap. Early American homes did not have indoor plumbing or bathrooms. A small building known as an outhouse, privy, or necessary, was located near the house. People also used a chamber pot in their bedroom so they didn't have to go to the outhouse at night.

Gardens and Orchards

Even with a small town lot, people could provide themselves with most of their own food. There was always plenty of work to do outside in the yard, tending the gardens, orchards, and berry patches.

Many colonists brought seeds with them from Europe in their journey across the ocean. From these seeds, early Americans planted herb, flower, and vegetable gardens. Thereafter, they saved seeds at harvest time. Or they swapped seeds with neighbors, because seeds were not sold in stores. People grew many garden crops that stored well, especially potatoes, cabbages, beans, carrots, turnips, and beets. They also planted greens, which were eaten fresh in salads during the summer. They grew many kinds of herbs, which were used for seasoning foods and making medicines.

Many people planted orchards of apple, pear, cherry, and plum trees. Grown in abundance, apples were used in many ways—pressed into apple cider, made into apple butter, and sliced and dried by the fire. Apples were baked fresh into pies or made into applesauce. The fruit also kept well in the cool cellar. When fresh apples were no longer available, women used the dried pieces in making pies and other dishes.

Beehives. Both the English and the Dutch imported bees, which Native Americans sometimes called "English flies." Nearly every household had a few hives of bees. These useful insects produced honey, which was used as a sweetener, and beeswax, which was used in making candles. As they collected nectar, the bees also spread pollen to orchard trees and garden plants. Colonists built hives of wood or woven straw, called skips, for their bees. The hives were usually placed on the south side of the house near gardens where the bees could easily collect nectar from blossoms and flowers.

Apples, which kept well, could be made into applesauce, apple cider, or apple butter, or baked into delicious pies.

Outbuildings

There were small buildings in the yard, sometimes called dependencies. These were used to house livestock and to prepare and store foods.

Root Cellars. Some homes had sloping doors outside that opened to a staircase that led down to a cool cellar. If not, the family had a separate root cellar in the yard. Here, they stored potatoes, carrots, apples, and other foods in straw or sand to keep them cool and dry. Many fruits and vegetables had to be eaten fresh or preserved. Berries and fruits were cooked with sugar to make preserves such as jams and jellies. These were placed in clay pots called crocks and stored in a corner of the cellar. Whole apples, pears, and root vegetables could simply be stored in the cellars, but others were pickled. Cabbage was made into sauerkraut and coleslaw, which was stored in crocks and kept in the cellar, too.

Barns and Sheds. Early Americans couldn't buy all their food at the general store, so even people who lived in villages kept animals. Pigs, chickens, sheep, and cows provided milk,

Outside doors led to a cellar under the house, where people stored apples, potatoes, and other vegetables through the winter.

Cattle, sheep, and horses were sheltered in small barns located in the yard not too far from the family home.

eggs, meat, wool, and tallow. Some people also kept a horse and sometimes one or two oxen. Chickens were housed in a coop. Coops had windows, facing south, since chickens laid more eggs if they had plenty of sunlight. Inside, they had perches, or roosts, and straw-filled nest boxes in which the hens laid their eggs. Pigs were penned in a shed called a pigsty. Other animals were sheltered in a small barn or stable. These buildings were situated close to the house so that people could easily care for the animals.

Among their many chores, women made butter by methodically plunging a wooden tool up and down in a churn filled with cream.

Smokehouses. Since early Americans didn't have refrigerators or freezers they preserved meat in the smokehouse. After butchering their hogs in the fall, people rubbed salt on the hams and hung them in the smokehouse along with slabs of bacon, rings of sausage, and other pieces of meat or fish. Smoke from a small fire filled the building and slowly cured the meat for a week or longer. Smoked meats kept well through the winter. The meats had a delicious flavor from the hickory, apple, or other kinds of wood used for the fire. Meat could also be pickled in crocks or preserved in barrels of salty water called brine. Early Americans used a lot of salt for preserving food. Salt works were established along the ocean coast to evaporate seawater. It was also mined from deposits found in the woods.

The Dairy. Many families kept at least one milk cow, which provided milk and cream. The fresh milk was taken to a small building called a dairy that was situated in a shady part of the yard. The dairy often had two rooms—one for making butter and cheese, and the other for storing these dairy products. It had a stone floor that helped to keep the inside cool. Just as families used eggs in many foods, they ate cheese and butter every day. People didn't trust water, which might make them sick, so they drank milk with every meal.

To make butter, girls and women first left a crock of milk overnight in a cool place in the dairy. The cream gradually rose to the top. In the morning, they skimmed the thick cream and poured it into a butter churn. The butter churn was a wooden barrel that narrowed at the top. A wooden pole, or dasher, stuck through the top. Girls methodically pumped the dasher up and down to stir the cream. This stirring slowly separated the butter from the liquid, or buttermilk. They dug the glob of yellow butter out of the churn, rinsed and lightly salted it, then shaped it in a mold. The term "butterfingers," meaning someone who tends to drop things, comes from handling slippery butter. The fresh buttermilk left in the churn was used for cooking and drinking.

Girls and women also made cheese in the dairy. They first curdled milk by separating the lumps called curds from the liquid called **whey**. The curds were sometimes eaten soft like cottage cheese or pressed together to make a hard cheese, which kept well for months.

A bowl of freshly churned butter took time and effort to make.

With four sides and a roof overhead, the well house protected fresh water from leaves and other debris.

Springhouses and Wells. Early American houses did not have running water for drinking, cooking, and washing dishes and clothes. People had to get their water from a spring or hand-dug well. If a family had a spring on their property, they constructed a small stone building over it. The springhouse protected the clear, cold water from falling leaves and other debris. They also stored milk and cheese inside to keep them cool. Kept in crocks, fresh milk could be placed right in the water.

If the family didn't have a spring, they dug a well in the yard. They lined the well with bricks or stones to keep earthen walls from caving in. They often built a roof over the opening. They covered the top with a round wooden lid to keep small children from tumbling into the well. When they needed water, they lowered a wooden bucket tied to a rope on a pulley. When the bucket was filled with water, they pulled it back up.

From Colonies to Young Nation

Life in an early American village was not easy. Many people worked as indentured servants or apprentices. However, after they had worked a few years, a servant was freed. Sometimes, a freed servant might receive a gift of land. However, most often, he or she could expect no more than "a year's provision of corn, double apparel, tools necessary." Yet young men, who had been apprenticed to a craftsman, often left with work skills or the chance to acquire farm land. In the colonies, men outnumbered women seven to one. So after her indenture, a woman easily found a husband. As one man said, "Comely or homely, strong or weak, any young woman was too valuable to be overlooked, and most could find a man with prospects."

For two hundred years, from the first settlements at Jamestown and Plymouth to the early 1800s, most people enjoyed their homes and communities. Working and playing together, they were able to provide themselves with the basics of food, clothing, and shelter. They were also able to have some comforts in life. Children learned in schools and craftsmen took pride in their work. Parents provided for their families, and everyone worked to build a good community for themselves and future generations.

After serving an apprenticeship for several years, a young man learned a craft that would enable him to make his way in the world.

Glossary

almanac—book about the weather and planting times for crops and practical advice

apprentice—person who learns a skill from another

broadside—advertising poster

cast-iron—metal that is heated to a liquid and poured, or "cast," into a mold

embroidery—stitching designs on cloth, leather, or paper

indenture—formal agreement in which one person works for another for a certain period of time

joiner—woodworker who joins pieces of wood together to make furniture

lathe—machine that turns wood and shapes it by cutting

livery stable—shelter for horses

lug pole—metal rod for hanging pots over the fire

meetinghouse—building used for religious worship and for town meetings

silhouette—side view of a person cut out of dark material and mounted against a light background

surveyor—person who makes exact measurements of land

tankard—tall mug usually made of metal

tanner—person who turns animal skins into leather

trenchers—dishes for serving food

turner—woodworker who uses a lathe to make rounded legs for tables and chairs

warming pan—long-handled pan of hot coals used to warm the sheets and blankets of a bed

whey—watery part of milk separated from curds in cheese making.

wrought iron—hand-worked iron

yoke—curved wooden collar used to harness two animals, usually oxen, to a plow or wagon

Time Line

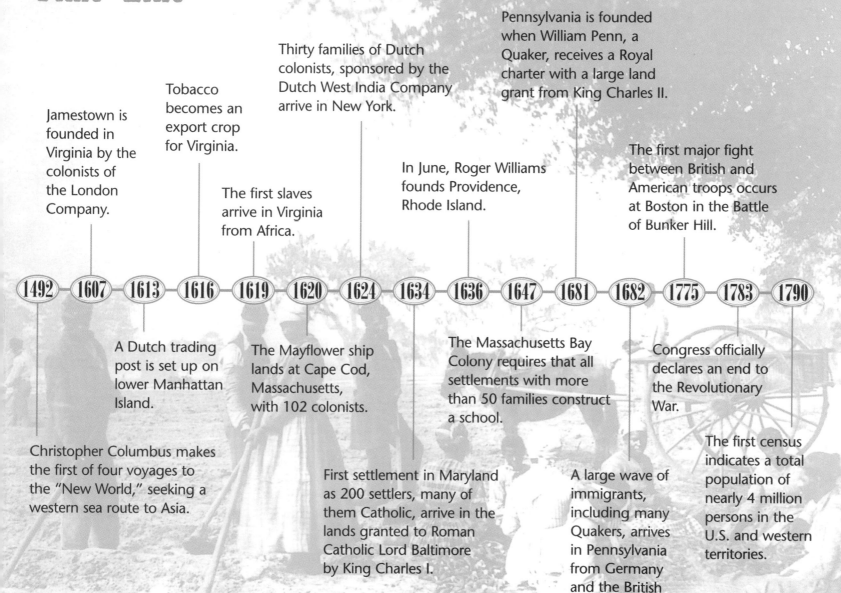

Jamestown is founded in Virginia by the colonists of the London Company.

Tobacco becomes an export crop for Virginia.

Thirty families of Dutch colonists, sponsored by the Dutch West India Company arrive in New York.

Pennsylvania is founded when William Penn, a Quaker, receives a Royal charter with a large land grant from King Charles II.

The first slaves arrive in Virginia from Africa.

In June, Roger Williams founds Providence, Rhode Island.

The first major fight between British and American troops occurs at Boston in the Battle of Bunker Hill.

1492 · **1607** · **1613** · **1616** · **1619** · **1620** · **1624** · **1634** · **1636** · **1647** · **1681** · **1682** · **1775** · **1783** · **1790**

A Dutch trading post is set up on lower Manhattan Island.

The Mayflower ship lands at Cape Cod, Massachusetts, with 102 colonists.

The Massachusetts Bay Colony requires that all settlements with more than 50 families construct a school.

Congress officially declares an end to the Revolutionary War.

Christopher Columbus makes the first of four voyages to the "New World," seeking a western sea route to Asia.

First settlement in Maryland as 200 settlers, many of them Catholic, arrive in the lands granted to Roman Catholic Lord Baltimore by King Charles I.

A large wave of immigrants, including many Quakers, arrives in Pennsylvania from Germany and the British Isles.

The first census indicates a total population of nearly 4 million persons in the U.S. and western territories.

Find Out More

Children's Books

Burt, Barbara. *Colonial Life: The Adventures of Benjamin Wilcox*. Washington, DC: National Geographic Society, 2002.

Cobb, Mary and Ellis, Jan Davey. *A Sampler View of Colonial Life*. Brookfield, CT: Millbrook Press, 1999.

Isaacs, Sally Senzell. *Life in a Colonial Town*. Chicago: Heinemann Library, 2001.

January, Brendan. *Colonial Life*. New York: Children's Press, 2000.

Kalman, Bobbie. *Colonial Life*. New York: Crabtree Pub. Co., 1992.

Kalman, Bobbie and DeBiasi, Antoinette. *Colonial Crafts*. New York: Crabtree Pub., 1992.

Kent, Deborah. *In the Middle Colonies*. New York: Benchmark Books, 1999.

Smith, C. Carter. *Daily Life: A Sourcebook on Colonial America*. Brookfield, CT: Millbrook Press, 1991.

Stefoff, Rebecca. *Colonial Life*. New York: Benchmark Books, 2002.

Wade, Linda R. *Life in Colonial America*. Edina, MN: Abdo Pub., 2000.

Warner, J. F. *Colonial American Home Life*. New York: F. Watts, 1993.

Wilmore, Kathy. *A Day in the Life of a Colonial Blacksmith*. New York: Newbridge Educational Pub., 2000.

Wilmore, Kathy. *A Day in the Life of a Colonial Innkeeper*. New York: Newbridge Educational Pub., 2000.

Wilmore, Kathy. *A Day in the Life of a Colonial Printer*. New York: Newbridge Educational Pub., 2000.

Wilmore, Kathy. *A Day in the Life of a Colonial Schoolteacher*. New York: Newbridge Educational Pub., 2000.

Places to Visit:

Colonial National Historical Park
P.O. Box 210
Yorktown, VA 23690
Phone: (757) 898–2410;
(757) 229–1733

Colonial Williamsburg
P. O. Box 1776
Williamsburg, VA 23187–1776
Phone: (757) 229–1000
www.falcon.jmu.edu/~ramseyil/colonial.htm

Historic Deerfield, Inc.
Box 321
Deerfield, MA 01342–0321
Phone: (413) 774–5581
www.historic-deerfield.org/index.html

Plimoth Plantation
P.O. Box 1620
Plymouth, MA 02362
Phone: (508) 746–1622
www.plimoth.org/ppinc.htm

Shelburne Museum
U.S. Route 7, P.O. Box 10
Shelburne, Vermont 05482
Phone: (802) 985–3346
www.shelburnemuseum.org/

Strawbery Banke Museum
P.O. Box 300
Portsmouth, NH 03802
Phone: (603) 433–1100
www.strawberybanke.org/

Selected Websites:

America's Stories from America's Library
www.americaslibrary.gov/cgibin/page.cgi/jb/colonial

Colonial America
www.members.aol.com/TeacherNet/Colonial.html

Colonial America
www.mce.k12tn.net/colonial_times/colonial_america.htm

Colonial America 1600–1775 K12 Resources
www.falcon.jmu.edu/~ramseyil/colonial.htm

Colonial American History and the Early Republic to 1812 Guide to Resources on the Web
www.web.uccs.edu/~history/index/colonial.html

Colonial National Historical Park
www.nps.gov/colo/

Old Salem
www.oldsalem.org/

Society for the Preservation of New England Antiquities
www.spnea.org/index.htm

Index

A

almanacs, *13*, 13–14
apples, 35
apprentices, 16, *17*, 18, 40–41
artisans, 14–17

B

barns, 36
barter, 12
bedchambers, 33
bees, 35
blacksmiths, *14*, 15
brickworks, 8
businesses, 12
butter and buttermaking, 39, *39*

C

cabinetmakers, 14, 28, 33
cabins, 26
candlemaking, *22*, 23
carpenters, 14
children, 21–22, 29
cooperative tasks, 11, 21–25
corn, 32
cottages, 4, 26
cow herder, 11

D

dairy buildings, 38–39

F

fence-viewers, 11–12
fires and fireplaces, 21, *30*, 30–31
flax, 22
food, 31–32, 38–39
    growing, 34–35
    preservation of, 36, 38
forests, 7–8
forts, 4
Franklin, Benjamin, 14
furniture, 28, 33, 34

G

games, 20
general stores, 12
gristmills, 8, *9*, 10

H

houses, 4, *5*, 26–27

J

Jamestown, Virginia, 4–5, 43

K

kitchens, 29–30

L

linen, *22*, 22
livestock, 36–37

M

mansions, 27
Massachusetts Bay Company, 43
meetinghouses, 10–11

N

New Netherland, 6
New York, 6
newspapers, 13

P

Penn, William, 6, 43
Pennsylvania, 6–7
Pilgrims, 6
plantations, 27
Plymouth, Massachusetts, 6
potters, 16
Puritans, 6, 25

Q

Quakers, 6, 43
quilts and quilt-making, *24*, 24–25

R

roofs, 26–27
root cellars, 36, *36*

S

salt, 38
saltbox houses, 26, *27*

S

sawmills, 8, *9*
schoolhouses, 19
schools, 18–21, 43
shepherds, 11
silhouettes, *28*, 28
smokehouses, 38
soapmaking, 23–24
social events, 25
springhouses, 40
sugar, 32

T

tankards, *31*
tanners, 16
tobacco, 6, 43
tools, 30–31
town crier, 14
trading for supplies, 12

U

utensils, 31

V

Virginia, 4, 43

W

water, getting, 40
wells, 40
windows, 28
women, 22–25, 29

About the Author

The author and illustrator of over eighty books for children and adults, **Raymond Bial** is best known for his versatility in portraiture, landscape, and still-life photography. His photo-essays for children include *Corn Belt Harvest, County Fair, Amish Home, Frontier Home, Shaker Home, The Underground Railroad, Portrait of a Farm Family, With Needle and Thread: A Book About Quilts, Mist Over the Mountains: Appalachia and Its People, Cajun Home, One-Room School, Where Lincoln Walked, Ghost Towns of the American West, A Handful of Dirt, Tenement: Immigrant Life on the Lower East Side*, and many others. His series of books include Building America and Lifeways, an acclaimed series about Native-American people. He has published three works of fiction for children: *The Fresh Grave and Other Ghostly Stories, The Ghost of Honeymoon Creek*, and *Shadow Island*. He lives in Urbana, Illinois, with his wife and children.